BUSHMEN OF SOUTHERN AFRICA

Galadriel Watson

WEIGL PUBLISHERS INC.

Published by Weigl Publishers Inc.
350 5th Avenue, Suite 3304, PMB 6G
New York, NY 10118-0069 USA
Web site: www.weigl.com

Library of Congress Cataloging-in-Publication Data

Watson, Galadriel Findlay.
  Bushmen of South Africa / Galadriel Watson.
    p. cm. -- (Indigenous peoples)
  Includes index.
  ISBN 1-59036-222-5 (lib. bdg. : alk. paper) 1-59036-254-3 (softcover)
  1. San (African people)--Juvenile literature. I. Title. II. Series.
  DT1058.S36W38 2005
  305.896'1--dc22

                              2004005774

Printed in the United States of America
1 2 3 4 5 6 7 8 9 0   08 07 06 05 04

Project Coordinator Heather C. Hudak **Design** Terry Paulhus **Layout** Katherine Phillips and Jeff Brown **Copy Editor** Janice L. Redlin **Photo Research** Wendy Cosh and Ellen Bryan

Consultant Megan Biesele, Ph. D.
                 Coordinator, Kalahari Peoples Fund

CONTENTS

Where in the World?

The Bushmen of southern Africa live in the Kalahari Desert of Namibia, Botswana, and Angola. Only about one-third of the Bushmen living in southern Africa continue to practice their traditional ways of life.

Some experts believe the Bushmen have lived in southern Africa for about 10,000 years. Others believe the Bushmen have lived in this area for as long as 40,000 years. Regardless of when they first arrived in southern Africa, the Bushmen lived during the time of the **Ice Age**. At this time, nearly one-third of the world was covered with ice.

The Bushmen once lived throughout southern and eastern Africa. Over time, European **settlers** and other African peoples forced them to an area where few others dared to live. This area was called the Kalahari Desert. Today, about 100,000 Bushmen live in and around the desert, primarily in the countries of Botswana, Namibia, and Angola.

Traditionally, the Bushmen lived as hunter-gatherers. This means they hunted animals for meat and gathered plants such as wild vegetables and fruit. However, over time, their traditional way of life has changed. For example, in the early 1900s, about 60 percent of the Bushmen lived as full-time hunter-gatherers. By 1976, less than 5 percent lived as

The Bushmen are the oldest inhabitants of southern Africa. They have lived as hunter-gatherers in this area for thousands of years.

hunter-gatherers. Other Bushmen worked as farm laborers or lived on government **settlements**, which offered financial support. Today, government **persecution** prevents many Bushmen from practicing their traditional ways.

The Bushmen do not look like other African peoples. Many Bushmen are lean and stand about five feet (1.5 meters) tall. They have sharp-featured faces, olive skin, and tightly coiled hair.

There are many Bushmen **bands**. Each band has a name, such as !Kung, !Xo, G/wi, or Kua. Each band may have different customs and practices, as well.

■ The Kalahari Desert covers more than 190,000 square miles (500,000 square kilometers), making this desert larger than the entire state of California, which is 185,869 square miles (411,469 square kilometers).

■ Summer temperatures in the Kalahari can reach up to 104° Fahrenheit (40° Celsius). In winter, night temperatures become frostier, dipping down to about 40° F (4° C).

■ Animals that call the Kalahari home include the hyena, antelope, lion, wildebeest, and many bird and reptile species.

■ Although the Kalahari does receive some rain, it is very difficult to find water. In some areas, there are seasonal streams and a few permanent springs. Many areas have no surface water. In these areas, there may be water buried deep beneath the sand.

Stories and Legends

Bushmen stories often illustrate how these people survive in their harsh environment. Some stories tell of how the Bushmen hunt or pay respect to the animals they kill. Other stories explain how to find food or water.

The Bushmen enjoy telling stories. As one of their most common forms of entertainment, storytelling can last for many hours. Bushmen storytellers describe hunts, events, and gatherings. Sometimes, they simply **gossip**. Full of drama, the storyteller may gesture broadly or imitate the sounds of birds and animals. Storytellers repeat the story many times.

One popular type of story is *n≠wasi o n!osimasi*, or "stories of the old people." Bushmen elders most often tell stories to fellow elders. These stories recount the days of long ago, when God walked upon Earth and animals were people. These stories are often horrific or ridiculous. The Bushmen think many of the stories are hilarious.

Many of the stories the elders tell are about Bushmen gods. For example, !Kung band members believe in a Great God. This god has eight different names. They also believe in a Lesser God, known as Kauha the trickster. Many stories tell about the adventures of Kauha and his family.

Other stories explore themes such as how the Sun first appeared or how death came to the world. Some stories explain how animals developed from humans. For example, the aardvark, or ant bear, developed when a human tried to escape pursuers by digging underground. After a while, his hands turned into claws, better suited to digging, and he became an aardvark.

Some Bushmen believe that if the shadow of a certain bird species is cast on a child, the child can become ill. If this happens to a baby, the Bushmen perform a detailed ritual, which they believe will help cure the child of the illness.

The Bushmen tell many stories about the ostrich, too. One story explains how the ostrich was once a **gemsbok** antelope.

According to Bushmen legend, the ostrich was once a gemsbok antelope. After seeing a Bushmen walking on two legs, the ostrich burned his front legs in a fire.

THE STORY OF THE TSODILO HILLS

The Tsodilo Hills are located in the Kalahari Desert. To many of the Bushmen, these hills are **sacred**. This is one Bushmen story about how the hills developed.

Many ages ago, there was a man with two wives. Unfortunately, he loved one wife more than the other, and this caused many problems. While fighting, the wife who was loved less got very angry with the husband and hit him hard upon his head. This caused a large wound. She then ran away into the desert.

The Great God saw this fight. He told the husband and his wives that since there was no peace among them he must turn them into stone. The husband became the largest hill, with the gash upon its face. The loved wife and her children became the group of hills in the center. The unloved wife became the smallest hill farther off in the distance.

Out of the Past

The Bushmen use petroglyphs, or rock art, to tell stories. Petroglyphs on cave walls in Zimbabwe illustrate stories of how the Bushmen lived when they first came to the area.

Although the Bushmen once called all of eastern and southern Africa home, today, they live only in and around the Kalahari Desert. There are many different reasons why the Bushmen moved to this area.

About 4,000 to 2,000 years ago, another group of peoples emerged in southern Africa. This group, called the Hottentots, was descended from the same ancestors as the Bushmen. The Hottentot culture was similar to Bushmen culture. The only difference between the two groups was that the Hottentots raised cattle instead of hunting and gathering like the Bushmen. The cattle competed with the wild game for grass. This forced the game to move to a new location. The Bushmen followed the animals.

In AD 200, another group of cattle herders, known as Bantu-speaking Africans, entered Bushmen territory. As the Bantu-speaking population increased, they gained control over more land for farming and grazing. This forced the Bushmen

In the 1600s, Dutch explorers docked their ships on the southern tip of Africa to replenish their food and water supplies. Africa was the midpoint on their voyage to India. This is when they first met the Bushmen.

TIME LINE

40,000-10,000 years ago There are early traces of the Bushmen living in Africa

4,000-2,000 years ago Hottentot cattle ranchers force the Bushmen to leave their territory

AD 200 Bantu-speaking Africans move south, also taking control over Bushmen territory

1652 The Dutch first settle in Africa, at the Cape of Good Hope

1700s Clashes between Europeans and the Bushmen escalate

1774 One European raid upon the Bushmen leaves 503 Bushmen dead and 241 captured

late-1800s The last Bushmen are pushed out of southernmost Africa

1955 The Bushmen population declines to about 50,000 people

1961 The Central Kalahari Game Reserve is established and offered as a place for the Bushmen to live in the traditional way

1986 The Government of Botswana starts a campaign to drive the Bushmen out of the Central Kalahari Game Reserve

1992 The Bushmen hold the first-ever regional conference on Bushmen peoples. Here they speak about issues such as education, health, social services, and jobs

to leave the area in search of wild game.

In the 1600s, European settlers arrived in the region. As the settlers explored inland, they invaded Bushmen territory. The settlers killed the wild game without the Bushmen's permission. Upset by the settlers' lack of respect for their culture and land, the Bushmen killed many Europeans.

With such anger between the two groups, the Bushmen needed to leave the area. The Europeans had stronger, more powerful weapons, such as guns. They went on **expeditions** to kill as many Bushmen as possible. They sold other Bushmen into **slavery**. By the end of the 1700s, there were so few Bushmen alive they could no longer fight for their land. The Bushmen retreated. By the late 1800s, the only land remaining for the Bushmen was the Kalahari Desert. The climate and terrain was so harsh in the Kalahari that no other group wanted to live there.

In 1650, the Bushmen population was larger than 300,000 people. By 1955, only about 50,000 Bushmen remained. Since then, the population has increased to about 100,000 people.

Bushmen bands do not have a chief or leader. Instead, all adults, both male and female, participate in decision-making activities. There are no rituals or events marking these discussions.

The Bushmen population is divided into groups called bands. Made up of relatives and friends, a band comprises several families. Each band has a husband, one or more wives, and children. Bands have about twenty to sixty people. There is no band chief or leader, although skilled hunters or older men may have influence over certain matters.

Each band has a territory covering up to 400 square miles (1,040 sq km). The territory is selected according to the availability of plants and animals to eat, trees for shade, shelter, wood, and water sources. Within this territory, the band travels from place to place when either food or water runs low. People also move from band to band, either through marriage, as a visitor, or in search of items to trade.

Men and women have daily activities they must perform. Men hunt animals. Women gather plants. Men prepare animal skins, later made into items such as clothes. Women make ostrich eggshell beads. Both males and females have equal power within the family and band. Both have the right to voice their opinions. Sometimes, they help do each other's activities, too.

South African governments, such as Botswana, continue to force Bushmen families to live in permanent villages.

Children are not required to take part in daily chores. The children usually spend their time playing and wandering freely, though never far from the village. Girls are usually about 14 years of age when they start helping to gather food. Boys are about 16 years of age when they participate in their first serious hunt.

All members of a Bushmen community live together in open camps. They do not have much privacy. Other band members can hear any conversation that is louder than a quiet whisper.

The Bushmen use huts to store supplies. People only live inside the huts during extreme weather conditions. All band members share the open space and can roam freely throughout the campsite.

THE SEASONS

There are two distinct seasons in the Kalahari. The rainy season extends from January to March. During this time, rain turns the desert green and many plants grow. A Bushmen band can live in one area for several weeks before the local supplies are exhausted.

The dry season takes place between December and April. This means colder temperatures and less plant food available to the Bushmen. During this time, the band may split into individual households, each seeking food in a separate part of the band's territory.

Communication

The languages the Bushmen speak are called *Khoisan* languages. These languages are distinct from other languages because of their unique clicking sounds.

Although there are many Bushmen languages, they can be divided into five general groups.

Since there is no English language equivalent to the Bushmen's clicking sounds, Khoisan words are written using letters and symbols from the English language alphabet. The following are a few of the most common words.

Often, the Bushmen tell stories while gathering around the campfire. Some of the Bushmen have scars on their legs from sitting too near to the fire.

The letter *o/* sounds like "tsk, tsk." This sound is created by pulling the tongue away from behind the top teeth.

The letter *o=* makes a soft popping sound. This sound is made by pulling the tongue away from the ridge behind the top teeth.

The letter *o!* sounds like a sharp pop. This sound is made by pulling the tongue away from the roof of the mouth.

The letter *o//* sounds like the English noise made to urge a horse to move. This sound is made by pulling the tongue away from the ridge behind the side teeth.

Most Bushmen languages did not have a written form until recently. For example, in 1989, **linguists** and other researchers helped the Ju/'hoan Bushmen create their own dictionary. This dictionary was published in 1994, and it is updated often. Today, there is also a Ju/'hoan/English dictionary, and Ju/'hoan children can read schoolbooks in their own language.

The Bushmen have little use for mathematics. For example, when asked how many children a person has, the parent may not know the correct number.

NAME GAME

In recent years, one of the Bushmen's biggest communication challenges has been deciding what to call themselves. Since there are so many Bushmen bands living in several different countries, many names have been used to refer to the Bushmen as a whole.

For example, in Zimbabwe, the Bushmen were called *Amasili* or *Batwa*. In Angola, they were sometimes referred to as *Kwankhala*. Dutch settlers used the name "Bushmen," but some Bushmen consider the term insulting. Others prefer the name "San," which is said to mean "bush dweller." However, others believe this name is also insulting. Some want to be called *N/oakwe*, or "red people." In Botswana, the Bushmen were most often called *Basarwa*, or "people of the south." In 1978, the Botswana government decided to call all rural people "Remote Area Dwellers."

To stop the confusion, in 1996, Namibian Bushmen representatives met and agreed to call themselves "San."

The Bushmen also do not have a system for keeping time, and they do not use the concept of years.

Throughout history, the Bushmen have used oral storytelling, song, and dance to pass their culture and traditions from one **generation** to another.

Law and Order

In general, the Bushmen avoid bad relations whenever possible. Although they are not a very generous culture, and sometimes they take part in dangerous quarrels, the Bushmen usually obey a set of unspoken **social laws**.

For example, the fair sharing of meat after a hunt is very important. The person who owned the arrow that killed the animal divides the meat among the band. Sometimes, the arrow owner did not take part in the hunt. Still, this person divides the meat. The meat is always divided equally, and no one eats more than a modest share.

Bushmen women welcome visitors who are invited to sit at a fire. To welcome the visitor, the woman takes a sweet-smelling powder from the tortoiseshell hung around her neck and sprinkles it over the visitor's head. This is just one of the many ways the Bushmen show good

Both women and men are considered equal in Bushmen culture. This is because the men hunt game to add to their diet, but the women gather much of the food that is used to prepare daily meals.

manners and keep order in their villages.

To receive food or a gift, Bushmen hold out both hands while the gift giver places the object in the receiver's hands. To hold out just one hand is considered grabbing and is, therefore, impolite. In addition, strangers always lay down their weapons when first meeting new people. Gossiping is also considered unacceptable behavior.

Rather than become aggressive when angry, the Bushmen usually talk about their problems. To teach the youth to hold their tempers, the Bushmen may try to repeatedly embarrass them by joking about their weaknesses.

When someone does not obey the rules, there are two main ways to bring the person back to order. First, the Bushmen may talk about the person. They may point out the poor behavior, gossip about the situation, or hint at the problem. Second, the Bushmen may sing about the problem to show their disapproval.

Marriage is another important aspect of Bushmen life. Marriage is arranged by parents. Often, the first marriage is unhappy, and

Bushmen boys and girls are equal in Bushmen culture. They begin sharing family and band responsibilities when they are about 16 years old. Boys begin hunting with the men. Girls help their mothers gather.

the couple divorces soon after the wedding. The man and woman then settle into new marriages. Some Bushmen marriages are **polygamous**.

Girls are often married as young as 7 years of age. However, these girls usually live with their parents until they reach **puberty**. Boys are usually about 14 years of age when they marry. Before they wed, boys must prove they can feed their families by performing their first successful hunt.

Celebrating Culture

Dancing is an important part of Bushmen life. The Bushmen dance after a birth, a marriage, sharing meat, a girl reaches puberty, or a boy's first kill in the hunt. Often, the Bushmen dance for fun. One of the most important reasons to dance is the *!kia* ceremony. This ceremony is performed by the !Kung.

The purpose of a !kia ceremony is to activate *n/um*. N/um is an energy that lies in the pit of the stomach. The Bushmen believe about one-half of Bushmen men and one-third of the women have n/um. They also believe n/um is **inherited**.

At the !kia ceremony, which usually lasts from dusk to dawn and takes place once or twice each week, the entire village gathers around a fire. The people at the center of the gathering sing and clap, while others dance around them. As a person dances, the

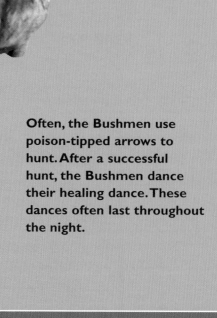

Often, the Bushmen use poison-tipped arrows to hunt. After a successful hunt, the Bushmen dance their healing dance. These dances often last throughout the night.

16

n/um heats up and becomes a vapor. This vapor then rises up the person's spine to the skull.

Once the n/um master is "in !kia," he or she can perform many tasks. The n/um master can help people with emotional concerns. This person can also see across long distances. The n/um master can use x-ray vision or walk on fire without becoming burned. A guardian watches over each n/um master to ensure there are no injuries.

One of the most important skills the n/um master has is the ability to heal. The Bushmen believe that a person becomes ill when dead ancestors choose to take the person to their realm.

When in !kia, the n/um master struggles and argues with the ghosts. If the n/um master loses the battle, the sick person may die. If he wins, the sick person becomes well.

Having many n/um masters benefits the community, so the Bushmen encourage young people to develop their n/um. To do so, the "students" attend many !kia dances. While at these dances, n/um masters guide the students into accepting their n/um. However, the pain of the rising n/um, as well as the student's fear of not returning from the !kia state, stops many from realizing their potential.

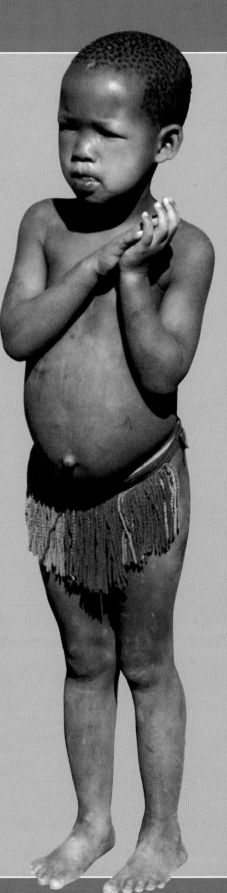

Bushmen children may encourage the n/um dance by singing and playing games around a fire. As the night progresses, children join their mothers in a circle around the fire while the men dance.

Art and Culture

Although the Bushmen do not record birthdays or anniversaries, they enjoy giving gifts for other occasions. They give gifts for **betrothals**, weddings, and a baby's first haircut. Sometimes, they give gifts even when they are not celebrating a special occasion.

Maintaining friendships is one of the main reasons the Bushmen exchange gifts. Nearly every item a person owns was given to him or her as a gift. These items may be given to someone else one day. The gifts are items the Bushmen use daily, such as a nicely shaped bowl or spoon carved of wood. The Bushmen take special care when making gifts because well-made items may be used for generations. The Bushmen do not spend much time decorating these items.

One art form the Bushmen practice is ostrich eggshell engraving. Hollow ostrich eggshells are used as containers, usually for carrying water. To engrave the shell, the artist scratches a design on its surface with a sharp knife. The artist then rubs the shell with **charcoal**, and the markings appear as black designs on the cream-colored shell.

Musical instruments are also an important part of Bushmen culture. The hunting bow is used as an instrument. Another instrument is the

During rainy periods, the Bushmen stored water in ostrich eggs. They buried the water-filled eggs in the ground for use in droughts. Today, ostrich eggs are most often used as decoration.

//gwashi. Traditionally, the Bushmen made this four-stringed instrument from a hollowed block of wood. They attached curved sticks and **sinew** strings to the wood. Today, the Bushmen make the //gwashi out of an empty food can.

The Bushmen also make other instruments, too. They make thumb pianos from flattened fencing wire and dance rattles from moth or butterfly **cocoons** that are filled with broken ostrich eggshells.

Today, the Bushmen make musical instruments from a variety of items. For example, some use cooking oilcans to make guitars.

PAINTING ON ROCKS

For thousands of years, the Bushmen practiced one art form called rock painting. This art still exists today.

The earliest Bushmen paintings are about 6,000 years old. They are located throughout the southern African landscape. The pictures show people singing, running, or dancing at the !kia ceremony. They also show the local wildlife. Later paintings depict the European settlers' ships and wagons, and British soldiers wearing uniforms.

To make the pictures, the Bushmen may have used paintbrushes made of feathers, wildebeest hair, or hollowed bones. They used white clay, charcoal, and ground stone for color.

After the Europeans and other Africans forced the Bushmen to move to the Kalahari Desert, the Bushmen had few rocks to paint. The only rocks were in the Tsodilo Hills, which the San believe the Great God himself painted. Today, no Bushmen rock painters remain.

Dressing Up

Once skinned, antelope hide is stretched out to dry. The Bushmen place the hairy side to the ground. Once processed, soft hide is cut into different shapes and sewn together.

After the Bushmen kill an antelope, the men stake the hide flat to dry. About 1 day later, they scrape the hide clean of fat using a sharp blade. If they plan to use the skin to make clothing, they scrape off the hair, as well. Then, the men rub the juice of a **Crinum bulb** all over the hide. They may repeat this process many times. The Crinum bulb juice **tans** the hide and makes it flexible.

The Bushmen sew the hides into clothing with threads of sinew and needles of bone or metal. Most men wear a **loincloth**. The women wear front and back aprons. They hang leather slings, called *karosses*, from their shoulders. They use karosses to carry food, belongings,

or infants. Today, the few Bushmen who still live in the traditional way may also wear tattered pieces of western clothing.

Ostrich eggshell beads are also important to the Bushmen. When an ostrich eggshell container breaks, the women gather the pieces, chop them into smaller circles, then punch holes into each piece. They string these beads onto sinew, creating long necklaces that reach to the belly button. They may also sew beads onto clothes, karosses, hunting bags, and headbands. Today, the Bushmen also use colorful glass or plastic beads, which they acquire through trade.

One way the men increase their attractiveness is by shaving their heads, creating a pattern in their hair. This also helps keep their hair free of dirt and pests.

Bushmen women carry skin bags for gathering plants.

BODY TALK

Both boys and girls are scarred for beauty and to mark certain rites of passage. For example, a boy is scarred on his face, arms, chest, and back after his first successful hunt. The scar is made by cutting the skin, then rubbing animal fat and plant **ash** into the cut. This ritual is performed on the right side of the boy's body if the animal was male and on the left side if the animal was female. The ritual is performed again after the boy kills an animal of the opposite gender. After receiving these scars, the boy is considered a man and is ready for marriage.

Girls are also scarred when they reach puberty. At this time, scars are placed on the back of each of the girl's shoulders and in the middle of her chest. The Bushmen also celebrate the occasion by dancing, painting their faces like a gemsbok, and dressing in beaded clothing, necklaces, and headbands.

Food and Fun

Bushmen mothers squeeze pounded tuber pulp to acquire moisture to wash their face and hands.

FINDING WATER

- Find a water-filled melon, tuber, or aloe plant to eat.
- Use a sipping stick to suck water from a hollow tree filled with rainwater.
- Use a sipping stick to suck water out of the sand.

Traditionally, the Bushmen are hunter-gatherers much like their ancient ancestors. Their diet consists mainly of plant matter, which is gathered by the women. The Bushmen eat about 150 types of plants, including wild vegetables such as **tubers**, fruits, and nuts. The //"*xa*, or *mongongo*, is an important food for the Bushmen. This fruit is widely available and has a nut of very high nutritional value.

Flying ants are a special treat the Bushmen eat. During a 2-day **infestation** of flying ants at the beginning of December, young women and children gather the insects. They collect thousands of the ants and roast them as food.

The men's job is to hunt. Antelope are very important, as well as other **herbivores**, such as wildebeest, *kudu*, and gemsbok. On average, a hunter kills about six large game every year. They usually kill these animals with poisoned arrows, or they catch the animals in a **snare**. The Bushmen eat about 100 animal species. They hunt warthogs with dogs, and they use fire to drive African porcupines out of their burrows. The big leopard tortoise is easy to catch. Cooked in its shell, the tortoise can be a large enough meal to feed an entire family.

Today, few of the Bushmen rely on their traditional ways of life. Instead, they work for their food.

As for entertainment, the Bushmen enjoy talking, singing, dancing, and smoking **tobacco**. They also play games. Games are not competitive because each band has a limited number of children and few of the same age, gender, and skill level.

The Bushmen do not play team sports. Rather than competing against each other, children try to better themselves by watching others practice a sport.

One game the Bushmen play is called *zeni* or *ahna*. During this game, the Bushmen throw a feather that is tied to a weight, such as a pebble or nut. The feather and the weight are the zeni. The goal is to catch the zeni before it lands, then hook a stick onto it and throw it back into the air. This is repeated until the zeni hits the ground.

Children also play make-believe. They imitate the adults by playing house and hunting or gathering food. Sometimes, they make dolls out of unused tubers. They may throw a melon as a ball. They may also throw sticks and see how far the sticks bounce.

Bushmen make whiplash snares to catch game birds.

Great Ideas

Visitors to the desert may not even notice a traditional Bushmen village until they stumble upon its huts. Bushmen huts are made of branches, twigs, and grass. They look like upside-down birds' nests. In fact, the Bushmen do not live inside their huts. Instead, they use the huts as storage containers for their belongings. The land between the circular village of the huts is used as an outdoor living area. During extreme rains or other weather conditions, the villagers may sleep inside the huts.

The Bushmen must be able to move their camp easily so they can search for food. As a result, they own few belongings. Some of these belongings are fire sticks.

To create fire, the Bushmen use their palms to quickly rub a piece of hardwood against a piece of softwood. The Bushmen place dry grass beneath the wood. The friction from rubbing the two pieces of wood together creates a fine dust that gathers

Many of the Bushmen now live as serfs who serve cattle ranchers. Serfs are people of the lowest rank who are forced to perform labor for others.

on the dry grass. When there is enough of this dust, the Bushmen blow on the grass until it bursts into flames.

The Bushmen also own bows and arrows. The bow is made of wood that is bound with sinew for extra strength. The bowstring is made of two thin sinew strings, which are removed from the long back muscles of a large antelope. The Bushmen weave the sinew together to make a very strong rope.

Traditionally, arrowheads are made of bone. Often, the Bushmen use an ostrich's shinbone to make arrowheads. Today, many arrowheads are made of metal. Using sinew strings, the Bushmen bind the arrowhead to a shaft of hollow reed, bone, and wood. These arrows are not strong enough to kill large animals. The Bushmen coat arrowheads with a deadly poison. Most often, this poison is made from the **larvae** of the chrysomelid beetle. The poison kills the animal, but not the person who eats the animal's meat.

The Bushmen are successful hunters because they use their observation skills to track animals. While hunting, they seek clues to lead them to animals. Bushmen hunters look at which direction hoofprints are pointing to determine which direction an animal is traveling. They look at the color of blood on the ground to learn when an animal was wounded and how long it will survive. They even consider the time of day and year when tracking an animal.

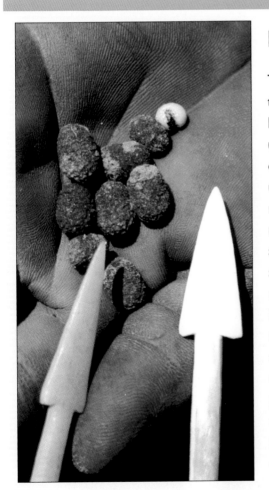

BEETLE POISON

The Bushmen use chrysomelid beetle poison to make their arrows more deadly. To obtain this poison, the Bushmen must first dig 1.6 to 3.3 ft (0.5 to 1 m) underground to unearth cocoons. Each cocoon has one larva inside. There are three methods the Bushmen use to poison their arrows with the larvae. After removing the larva from the cocoon, the Bushmen may squeeze its poison onto the arrowhead. They may apply the poison from as many as ten beetles to one arrow. Once the Bushmen have applied the poison, they may dry the arrows over a fire. Another method the Bushmen use is to mix beetle larvae with plant juices and saliva. They apply this mixture to the arrows. The third method is to dry the beetle larvae in the Sun. Once they are dried, the Bushmen grind the larvae into a powder. They mix the powder with plant juices and apply the mixture to the arrows. Over time, the beetle poison becomes less deadly. However, the poison remains strong enough to kill large game for up to 1 year.

At Issue

Today, only a small number of Bushmen still live in the traditional way. Some of the Bushmen were forced off their land and placed in government settlements that are unsuitable for hunting-gathering. Others have lost their territories to cattle ranches or game reserves. Some of the Bushmen left their land to make **boreholes** in times of drought. They decided not to return to hunting-gathering.

Many of the Bushmen live on ranches, working for food, water, and shelter rather than money. Others raise their own crops and livestock. Some receive financial assistance from governments and international aid agencies. Others work as soldiers in the government's army.

Many of the Bushmen live in poverty. Poor health is common, especially HIV/AIDS, as well as boredom, depression, alcoholism, and domestic violence. It is difficult for the Bushmen to receive

Most of the water in Botswana comes from boreholes. Boreholes are holes drilled deep into the ground. The Botswana government has drilled boreholes in the Kalahari Game Reserve.

medical attention, find jobs, or take advantage of business opportunities.

Some tourists to the Kalahari claim to have seen the Bushmen living in their traditional way. Often, these Bushmen have been hired from the villages to wear their traditional clothing and show the tourists how to find water-filled tubers or catch an ostrich. At the end of the working day, these Bushmen remove the skins, slip on their modern clothing, and return to their villages.

THE CENTRAL KALAHARI GAME RESERVE

The Central Kalahari Game Reserve was formed by the Botswana government in 1961. The reserve land was established to allow the Bushmen to continue their traditional hunting-gathering lifestyle. The reserve was closed to the public, and about 1,000 Bushmen began living on the land.

In 1986, the government of Botswana decided to remove the Bushmen from the reserve. For years, the government tried to make the Bushmen leave the area. In 1997, the government began forced removals from the reserve. At this time, the government placed about three-quarters of the reserve's population in settlements located outside the reserve. In 2002, the government destroyed the reserve's only borehole and banned hunting/gathering. Nearly the entire Bushmen population are now living away from the reserve. As of October 2002, about seventy Bushmen remained on the reserve, though many wished to return. Safari lodges and diamond mines are being constructed on the reserve.

In response, the Bushmen and other organizations are **lobbying** the government of Botswana, as well as political leaders around the world, in hopes of returning the reserve to the Bushmen.

Into the Future

Returning to the traditional way of life is not an option for most of the Bushmen. Instead, they are working to make a living in today's technological society.

Most Bushmen children attend school. Some schools teach these children in the Khoisan languages. However, many children must travel far from home to reach the schools. Often, few jobs await them when they graduate from school. Some of the Bushmen own small businesses. Others work in tourism.

Many of the Bushmen want land of their own. The only band to have recognized land rights is the =Khomani of South Africa.

To improve their status, the Bushmen are actively involved in politics. For example, since Botswana gained **independence** from Britain in 1966, many of the Bushmen vote during elections. In some cases, the Bushmen must walk great distances to reach the election polls. They may face harsh treatment when they arrive at the polls. Still, many participate in these elections.

In 1989, three Bushmen were elected onto a district council in one Botswana district. In 1994, seven more were elected onto a district council. In 1999, one of the Bushmen was elected to the House of Chiefs as a sub-chief.

The first conference on the Bushmen peoples was held in 1992. At this meeting, Bushmen representatives

Today, many of the Bushmen wear western-style blankets rather than traditional skin cloaks.

gathered to talk about subjects such as education, health, jobs, and land. The governments of Botswana and Namibia also attended and pledged their commitment to help the Bushmen.

Many projects, funded by religious groups, individuals, or, in some cases, the government, are helping the Bushmen support themselves. One such group, the Kalahari Peoples Fund, offers local-language educational programs and curriculum, as well as financial assistance for initiatives such as job training, **handicraft** grants, and even soccer team uniforms.

Since 1985, Botswana authorities have forced thousands of Bushmen peoples from their homes on the Central Kalahari Game Reserve. The Bushmen are being relocated to settlements outside the reserve.

THE DESERT'S DIET DRUG

In a decision that may affect indigenous peoples around the world, the South African San Council recently reached an agreement with South Africa's Council for Scientific and Industrial Research (CSIR).

For centuries, the Bushmen have used the Hoodia cactus to suppress hunger and thirst on hunting trips. It was this knowledge that lead the CSIR to start researching the cactus. The CSIR **patented** the active molecule within the cactus with no intention of sharing the profits with the Bushmen. It was only after a 3-year legal battle that the Bushmen won the right to protect, own, and profit from their indigenous knowledge.

The drug may be marketed in 2008, earning the Bushmen millions of dollars. The money will be put into a trust to be spent on education, skills development, and job creation.

Fascinating Facts

- Children of the Kua band are named after an event that happened around the time of their births.

- Bushmen women walk a total of about 1,500 miles (2,400 km) a year searching for food. This is equal to the distance between New York City and Miami.

- Fifty percent of Bushmen children die before adulthood.

- For about 300 days each year, the ≠Kade Bushmen cannot find water. They must obtain it from plants and animals.

- The Kalahari Desert is covered with grasses and trees. It is considered a desert because it has no permanent surface water.

- The Central Kalahari Game Reserve is the largest game reserve in the world.

- Bushmen men sometimes dress as ostriches to become nearer to wild animals while hunting.

- A Bushmen arrow can only travel a distance of about 75 feet (23 m), the length of a long garden hose.

- Bushmen hunters sometimes use fire to chase a lion from its kill. The hunters then take the kill for themselves.

- In Namibia, the South African Defense Force employs more of the Bushmen than any other employer. Aside from training for military operations, the Bushmen soldiers spend time on community development.

FURTHER READING

Biesele, Megan, and Kxao Royal /O/oo. *San*. New York: The Rosen Publishing Group, Inc., 1997.

Taylor, Jane, and Laurens van der Post. *Testament to the Bushmen*. New York: Viking, 1984.

WEB SITES

Kalahari Peoples Fund www.kalaharipeoples.org

Survival International www.survival-international.org/bushman.htm

Glossary

ash a powdery substance left behind when something is burned

bands groups of people who are related in some way

betrothals when people promise to marry other people

boreholes deep holes drilled to release groundwater

charcoal a black substance produced when wood is burned; also called coal

cocoons protective coverings for insect larvae

Crinum bulb the bulb of a plant with strap-shaped leaves and flowers that grows in warm regions

expeditions journeys taken by people who have a specific plan

gemsbok a type of large antelope

generation a group of people who are born at about the same time and who have many things in common

gossip chatty conversation about rumors or facts

handicraft crafts made by hand

herbivores plant-eating animals

Ice Age a cold period when ice sheets covered much of Earth

independence to gain freedom from the control of another country

infestation when a large number of unwanted creatures are found in one place

inherited received from a relative or friend

larvae the wingless, worm-shaped forms of certain young insects

linguists people who study languages

lobbying trying to influence a government's decisions

loincloth a cloth that covers the hips

patented when an organization or person is allowed to be the only one to make or sell a particular item

persecution when a group of people is treated cruelly

polygamous having more than one husband or wife

puberty the stage of life when a child becomes an adult

sacred worthy of respect

settlements areas set aside by a government to house a certain group of people

settlers people who come to live in a new place

sinew the tissue that attaches muscle to bone; also called a tendon

slavery the act of being forced to work for someone

snare a trap for small animals

social laws unwritten rules that guide how people behave

tans makes an animal hide into leather

tobacco special plant leaves that are dried and smoked

tubers the fleshy, swollen part of underground roots or stems, for example, a potato

Index

Photograph Credits

Every reasonable effort has been made to trace ownership and to obtain permission to reprint copyright material. The publishers would be pleased to have any errors or omissions brought to their attention so that they may be corrected in subsequent printings.

Cover: Ariadne Van Zandbergen/ Africaimagelibrary.co.za; **Corel Corporation:** page 7T; **Mary Evans Picture Library:** page 9; **Heather C. Hudak:** page 22B; **Peter Johnson/CORBIS/MAGMA:** page 7B; **Photos.com:** pages 4T, 6T, 8T, 10T, 12T, 14T, 18T, 20T, 22T, 24T, 26T, 28T; **D.C.H. Plowes:** pages 1, 3, 5, 6B, 8B, 10B, 11T, 11B, 12B, 13, 14B, 15, 16, 17, 18B, 19T, 19B, 20B, 21T, 21B, 22M, 23, 24B, 25, 26B, 27, 28B, 29T, 29B, 30.

On the cover
Older Bushmen children often build their own huts next to their parents' homes.